THE BASIC FIRE SAFETY HANDBOOK

DR. BENARD LANGO
Researcher & Published Author | Public Safety Management Lecturer | Research Mentorship & Training Coach
Dip. CS, Bsc. (IT), MA. PPM, PhD. PM

BENLANGO PUBLISHERS
NAIROBI, KENYA

Published By:
DR. BENARD LANGO RESEARCH SCHOOL
NAIROBI, KENYA

Printed By:
DR. BENARD LANGO RESEARCH SCHOOL
NAIROBI, KENYA

PREFACE

This handbook covers the basics of elementary fire safety at the school place and aims at imparting basic skills to young and old, primary and secondary level, young learners in fire safety field, and school decision makers who require basic knowledge in fire safety.

I am hopeful and confident that the pupils, students and teachers alike will find this book a useful aid to better understanding of fire safety skills. The suggestion for improvement and constructive opinion will be highly appreciated.

JULY 2014   **DR. BENARD LANGO**

CONTENTS

1.0 FORWARD

Schools and workplaces have in recent days seen major fires that were either avoidable or controllable with basic knowledge on fire safety and the right equipment. Fire safety education in most countries is not embedded in the curriculum and one only gets to learn about fire safety after completion of basic education, in most instances. This book therefore targets school and workplaces to embrace fire safety tradition by providing a well laid out steps in understanding the basics in fire safety in schools and workplaces and what to do in case of fire.

1.1 Students & Teachers responsibilities with regard to fire safety

It is the duty of all occupants to a building to familiarize themselves with escape routes from rooms that they normally use. Whether in the staffroom, classrooms, dormitory or hostels, or offices the students should note the following:

1. It is an offence to tamper with the firefighting equipment
2. Do not block the escape routes from dormitories or the stairwells.
3. Never store combustible materials (such as mattresses) next to escape routes.
4. Keep fire doors closed under normal circumstances. These doors should open in the direction of exit.

2.0 SAFETY ACTS IN KENYA RELATED TO FIRE SAFETY

Work Injury Benefits Act (WIBA) and the Occupational Health and Safety Administration (OSHA) Act 2007 stipulates many requirements that must be fulfilled by employers. Workplaces complying with the WIBA 2007 and OSHA 2007 have minimal exposures. The fire safety rules legal notice number 59 provides guidelines on occupational fire safety and the workplaces and provides the following guidelines:

2.1 Formation of firefighting teams:

Every occupier shall establish a firefighting team that shall consist of—(a)at least two persons, where the number of workers is not more than ten;(b)at least three persons, where the number of workers is between eleven and twenty five;(c)at least five persons, where the number of workers is more than twenty five.

2.2 Training in fire safety:

(1) Every occupier shall ensure that all workers are instructed in the safe use of fire fighting appliances.(2)The Minister may, on the advice of the Director, prescribe a basic training course on fire safety to be undertaken by every member of the fire fighting team.(3)The Minister may, on the advice of the Director, publish once every year, in the Gazette, a list of approved institutions for the training of the fire fighting team.(4)Every occupier shall ensure that every member of the firefighting team undertakes the basic fire safety training course within three months from the date of appointment into the firefighting team.(5) Every occupier shall cause every member of the firefighting team to undergo a firefighting refresher course at least once in every two years.

2.3 Functions of firefighting team

Firefighting team shall carry out the following functions—(a)ensure that all firefighting appliances, fire detection systems, fire alarm and any other facility for fire safety are in place and are regularly serviced;(b)conduct fire drills at the workplace;(c)investigate fire incidences at the workplace and recommend corrective measures;(d)regularly inspect the workplace for purposes of identifying potential fire risks and recommend remedial measures,(e)train other workers in the safe use of firefighting appliances;(f)co-ordinate the evacuation of other workers in the event of a fire; and(g)undertake any other functions as may be directed by the occupier.

In order to ascertain a safe school or college or a workplace, the following documents are mandatory requirements and they show the completion of a process:

- Certificate of workplace registration
- Workplace Fire safety policy
- Workplace fire drill report
- Workplace notice of fire occurrence report
- Workplace Fire safety audit report

3.0 CLASSIFICATION OF FIRE

It is usually important to understand different classifications of fire or the different types of fire. Fire is classified according to the type of fuel that is burning and if the wrong type of extinguisher is used, then this may lead to more dangerous situations.

The types of fire – The 5 five classifications of fire

Class A

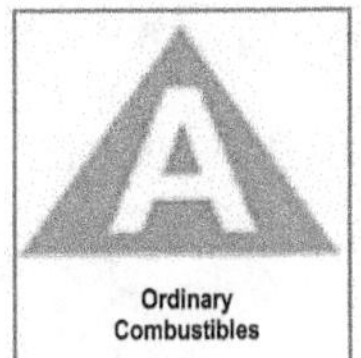

Class A type fires involve combustible materials like wood, paper, textiles, straw, coal, car tyres. They are often found in commercial and home buildings.

Class B

Class B type fires are caused by combustion of liquids or materials that liquefy for example fats, oils, petrol, paints alcohol and paraffin.

Class C

Class C type fires are caused by combustion of gases for example: hydrogen, natural gas, methane, propane and acetylene. Also Electrical—energized electrical equipment. As long as it's "plugged in."

Class D

Class D fires involve combustible metals such as sodium, magnesium, aluminium, lithium and potassium. These types of fires require special fire extinguishers.

Class F

Class F fires involve combustible oils and grease commonly found in commercial kitchens. The new cooking formulations used for commercial food preparation require a special wet chemical extinguishing agent that is specifically suited for extinguishing these hot fires that have the ability to re-flash. Never use other pressurized extinguisher types, as water, foam, powder or CO2 on burning cooking oil, as the pressure jet might carry the burning oil and spread the fire!

Not all fuels are the same, and if you use the wrong type of fire extinguisher on the wrong type of fuel, you can, in fact, make matters worse. It is therefore very important to understand the four different classifications of fuel.

4.0 THE FIRE TRIANGLE

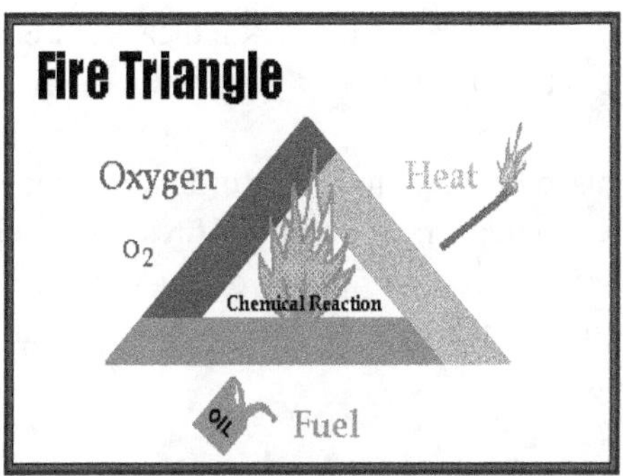

Fire Safety, at its most basic, is based upon the principle of keeping fuel sources and ignition sources separate. These three components form the **Triangle of Fire.** This representation was acceptable for a long time; meanwhile, many anomalous phenomena produced during a fire cannot be completely explained by this triangle.

A union sustained by these three elements, leads to the fourth element, the **Chain reaction,** which is produced in a continuous manner. The various components of the fire triangles are explained as:

- **Fuel**: All and any type of substance, which in the presence of oxygen and activation energy is capable of burning.
- **Oxygen**: It is the gas, that when present, causes fuel to burn, in its general form oxygen is considered a typical oxidizing agent found in normal air.
- **Heat**: It is the source of energy that when manifested in the form of heat can provoke the ignition of combustibles.

Considering the fire triangle, the various methods of extinguishing fire are described as:

- **Cooling**: This is the process of extinguishing fire by removing the heat element. By using water to put out fire from a burning house, it's the heat element from the triangle that is eliminated as oxygen and fuel is still there.
- **Smothering**: This is the removal of the fuel element. By withdrawing burning wood from a pot fire is reducing the wood on fire and slowly, the fire will reduced and finally burnout.
- **Starvation**: This process involves the elimination of oxygen from the reaction. When cooking and the oil in the cooking pot accidentally catch fire, you will close it with a lid to eliminate any more oxygen and this is the starvation process.

5.0 PORTABLE FIRE EXTINGUISHERS

Portable fire extinguishers are classified to indicate their ability to handle specific classes and sizes of fires. Labels on extinguishers indicate the class and relative size of fire that they can be expected to handle.

Class A extinguishers are used on fires involving ordinary combustibles, such as wood, cloth, and paper. Class B extinguishers are used on fires involving liquids, greases, and gases. Class C extinguishers are used on fires involving energized electrical equipment. Class D extinguishers are used on fires involving metals such as magnesium, titanium, zirconium, sodium, and potassium.

Fire Extinguishers are classified according to the extinguishing agents that are stored inside.

There are five extinguishing agents that are stored in fire extinguishers namely:

- **Water**
- **Co2**
- **Foam**
- **Dry powder**
- **Halogen**

Only four out of these are used because halogen has an effect on the ozone layer.

Extinguisher Original Color Coding

Before 1997, the entire body of the *fire extinguisher* was *color coded* according to the type of extinguishing agent:

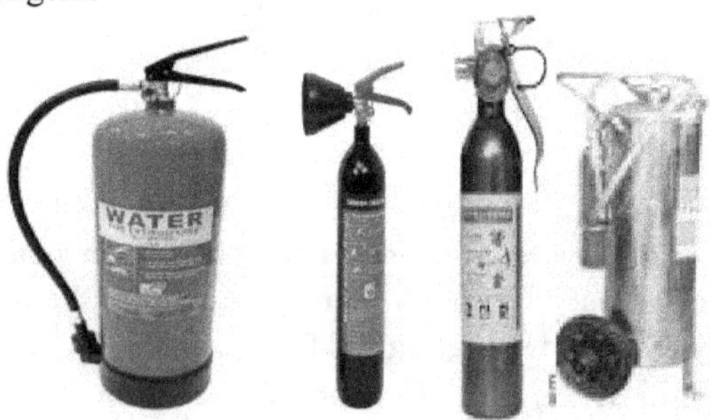

Extinguisher Revised Color Coding

The current color coding maintains 5% of the original color on all extinguishers hence currently the extinguishers will look like these:

Next time you see a fire extinguisher you will be able to differentiate whether it is an old type or the new model. Let's now discuss the each of the fire extinguishers:

5.1. Water Fire Extinguishers

APWs extinguish fire by taking away the "heat" element of the Fire Triangle.

APWs are designed for Class A fires only: Wood, paper, cloth.

- Using water on a flammable liquid fire could cause the fire to spread.
- Using water on an electrical fire increases the risk of electrocution. If you have no choice but to use an APW on an electrical fire, make sure the electrical equipment is un-plugged or de-energized.

5.2. CO2 Fire Extinguishers

CO_2s are designed for Class B and C (Electrical Sources) fires only!

CO_2s will frequently be found in laboratories, mechanical rooms, kitchens, and flammable liquid storage areas. In accordance with NFPA regulations (and manufacturers' recommendations), all CO_2 extinguishers must undergo hydrostatic testing and recharge every 5 years.

Carbon dioxide is a non-flammable gas that takes away the oxygen element of the fire triangle. Without oxygen, there is no fire. CO_2 is very cold as it comes out of the extinguisher, so it cools the fuel as well. A CO_2 may be ineffective in extinguishing a Class A fire because it may not be able to displace enough oxygen to successfully put the fire out. Class A materials may also smolder and re-ignite.

5.3. Dry Chemical Fire Extinguishers

Dry chemical extinguishers put out fire by coating the fuel with a thin layer of dust. This separates the fuel from the oxygen in the air. The powder also works to interrupt the chemical reaction of fire. These extinguishers are very effective at putting out fire.

"ABC" fire extinguishers are filled with a fine, yellow powder. The greatest portion of this powder is composed of monoammonium phosphate. The extinguishers are pressurized with nitrogen. Dry chemical extinguishers come in a variety of types…You may see them labeled:
- DC (for "Dry Chemical")
- ABC (can be used on Class A, B, or C fires)
- BC (designed for use on Class B and C fires)

5.4. Foam type fire extinguisher

AFFF Foam Extinguishers are suitable for use on Class A & B Fires. Foam extinguishers are especially good for use on material fires that are caused by wood, paper and textiles, cooling the flame by evaporation of the water in the foam. Good at combating flammable gases, as the foam creates a barrier between the flame and fuel.

Another good feature of the AFFF Foam Fire Extinguisher range is that the substance is non toxic and will not damage most materials.

Has a spray nozzle that covers a wide area when used, successfully coating the flame in a matter of seconds.

5.4.1 How do AFFF Foam Extinguishers work?

Foam Fire Extinguishers provide a fast, powerful means of tackling flammable liquids. They do so by creating a blanket of foam that smothers the fire, cutting of its supply of oxygen of oxygen and contains the flame preventing re-ignition.

5.4.2 Where are AFFF Foam Extinguishers most suitable for use?

AFFF Foam Fire Extinguishers are very popular for Homes, Flats, Cars, Caravans, HGV's & Boats.

Being suitable for use on Class A Fires, which includes Wood, Paper & textiles they are ideal for offices.

The Small 2 Ltr extinguishers are ideal for use in Cars and Caravans as they are small and compact. The 2 Ltr AFFF Foam is supplied with a mounting bracket which makes installation easy.

5.4.3 How Do You Identify a Foam Fire Extinguisher?

Foam Fire Extinguishers are easily identifiable by their Cream Label, as seen in the below image. There main body should be Red, to conform with British Standards, and they should have a Large Cream Banner across the top on the front of the extinguisher with Red writing stating "Foam".

Foam fire extinguishers that are manufactured to BS EN 3 should have a red body (RAL 3000) and a cream band covering 5-10% of the fire extinguishers surface area.

Old Foam Fire Extinguishers will have an entire Cream Body.

These no longer comply with British Standards and should be disposed of in an environmentally friendly manner.

5.5 Up close and Personal with a fire extinguisher

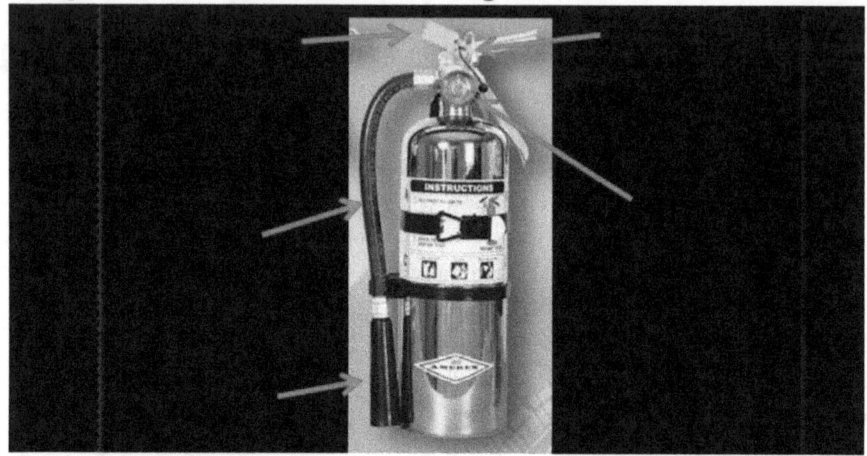

5.5.1. Pressure Gauge

5.6. How to use a fire extinguisher

Remember the word PASS which explains the use as follows:

- **P**ull the pin on the fire extinguisher handle to allow discharge.
- **A**im the nozzle/horn of the extinguisher at the base/bottom of the fire.
- **S**queeze the handles together to make the extinguisher work.
- **S**weep the nozzle/horn of the extinguisher from side to side as if using a broom.

Always verify the extinguishers before use, if they are adequate for the type of fire according to the extinguishing agent. Extinguishers with a normal charge of more than 3 kg or 3liters should be fitted with a discharge hose and nozzle the length of which should be less than 80% of that of the extinguisher body. The hose should not be under pressure until the extinguisher is operated.

5.7. Classification of fire extinguishers

Portable extinguishers can be divided into two groups:

- *Stored pressure type*: The expellant is stored with the extinguishing medium in the body of the extinguisher

- *Gas cartridge type*: The pressure is produced by the means of compressed liquefied gas is released from gas cartridge which is fitted into the extinguisher.

6.0 COMMON FIRE EQUIPMENT

There are common fire equipments in our everyday institutions, organizations and houses. This is an illustration of the common equipments, their uses, advantages and disadvantages.

6.1. SMOKE DETECTORS

It is common practice in modern-day living to install fire indicators into households, commercial, and industrial settings for the safety of the occupants. The size and type of a fire detector is dependent upon the setting (for example, smoke alarms in a household environment will indicate the presence of smoke by flashing a light or sounding a local alarm; whereas, mass smoke alarms that are installed in industry will connect a signal to a fire alarm system).

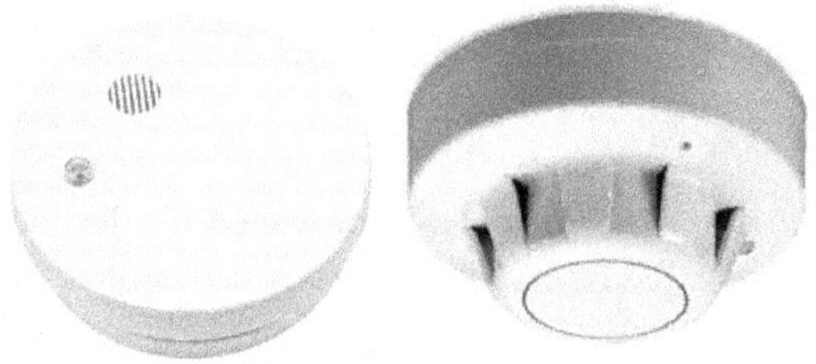

A typical house smoke detector is a disc shape powered by a disposable battery. There are two types of smoke detectors that work by either ***photoelectric detection***, or ***ionization***.

6.1.1 Photoelectric Smoke Detectors

A photoelectric smoke detector is a light detector with a light beam and electrical photocells (photodiodes) to track smoke particles. The light beam - made of incandescent build or an infrared LED light which helps collect the light source into a beam - in the smoke detector will reflect onto the photocells. The photocells in the sensing chamber are designed and arranged at a right angle to the beam of light in the chamber so that the light entering the chamber does not typically attract the photocells. When smoke particles enter the optical chamber, these particles interfere with the light beam (i.e., the lights reflects off the smoke particles) and then makes contact with the electrical photocells which increases the electrical charge in the detector to a threshold level that initiates an alarm signal.

Beam detectors are typically installed in large commercial and social settings including gymnasiums and auditoriums. Small household settings also use standard photoelectric smoke sensors. Optical alarms work well to detect slow-burning smoke fires.

Advantages
- Ideal for detecting dense smoke.
- Less prone to nuisance/false alarms generated from cooking fumes and shower steam.
- Does not contain radioactive material making these smoke detectors safer for use.

Disadvantages
- Sensitive to dust particles and insects which means that maintenance of optical smoke alarms becomes an issue.
- Expensive to maintain.
- Require more current to operate (they are typically wire to 110-volt power source).

Obscuring the light beam in a typical optical sensor is achieved in two ways:
- Light-obscuring method

Dense smoke distracts only part of the light beam, whereas less-dense smoke particles will be able to move around to obscure more of the light beam thus impacting the alarm system. In some instances, a mirror is used to position the light beam over a path which helps measure the area of coverage of the smoke particles.
- Light-scattering principle

A light scattering principle is based on the idea that smoke particles entering the sensing chamber strikes the light beam and scatters the light onto photoelectric particles.

6.1.2. Ionizing Smoke Detector

The Ionizing smoke detector is at a disadvantage to the optical smoke detectors because they use radioisotopes, such as americium-241 that ionizes smoke particles in the air.

Function principle to the radioactive isotope americium-241 involves emission of alpha particles that ionize air particles in the sensing chamber so that they conduct electricity. During emission of the alpha particles into air, a chemical reaction occurs whereby air molecules in the collecting chamber are ionized by the alpha particles and, as a result, carry an electrical charge. Smoke particles surrounding the ionizing smoke detector enter the collecting chamber and attach to the ions making it more difficult for the ions to deliver an electrical charge. A decrease in the electrical flow is detected by a circuit that then triggers an alarm system. This type of smoke detector is ideal for detecting invisible particles produced by flaming fires and so will work much faster and be more sensitive to detect smoke compared to a photoelectric detector.

6.2. HEAT DETECTORS

Heat detectors are the oldest and least expensive type of automatic fire detection. They are designed to operate when there is a specified or predetermined rate of temperature change or when a detecting element reaches a predetermined fixed temperature. The two types of heat detectors are spot and line type.

A spot type heat detector monitors temperature at a given point. These detectors vary with respect to the mechanisms used to detect heat. The two most common types of spot type heat detectors are:

6.2.1 Fixed-Temperature Heat Detectors:

These are designed to initiate an alarm when its heat sensitive material or element is heated to a specific temperature. The air temperature at the time of alarm is considerably higher as it takes time for the surrounding air to raise the temperature of the element to its set point. The operating range of these detectors start at 100F. There are two types of fixed-temperature heat detectors:

- o Restorable - returns to its ready state without any interaction from an outside source, once it has cooled below its set point.
- o Non-Restorable - requires replacement of its element after actuation.

6.2.2 Rate-of-Rise Heat Detectors

These operate on a rate-of-temperature change per unit of time basis. This type of heat detector contains a chamber with a calibrated vent. When the air in the chamber expands faster than it can escape from the vent, the increase in pressure causes the electrical contacts to close sending a signal to the fire alarm control unit. If the air in the chamber rises slowly and can escape from the vent, the electrical contacts do not close and there is no alarm.

Other types of spot detectors are:

- Rate-compensated heat detector
- Combination heat detector
- Pneumatic heat detector

Line type heat detectors are used in applications where it is not practical to use spot type detectors, such as on long industrial conveyors or cable trays. These detectors use heat-sensitive materials which affect the current flow through the electrical conductors.

6.3 FIRE BLANKETS

A **Fire Blanket** is a highly flame-resistant blanket that can be used to either extinguish a small fire or to wrap around a person. They are made from 2 layers of woven glass fibre fabric and an inner layer of fire retardant film. They work by cutting off the oxygen supply (oxygen is one of the three elements that a fire needs to burn) and smothering the fire.

6.3.1 HOW TO USE A FIRE BLANKET

It is **VITAL** that you know the correct way of using a *fire blanket* should you ever have to do so in an emergency at work or at home.

- Firstly, and most importantly turn off the gas or electricity supply.
- Remove the fire blanket from its container and hold it by the fabric straps
- To prevent burns on the hands and arms, make sure you wrap the top edges of the blanket around your hands to protect them.
- Roll up your sleeves so they do not catch in the flames.
- Carefully cover the flames with the fire blanket, making sure that you cover the whole area so that you can effectively cut off the airflow and extinguish the flames.

- However, If the fire is larger than the blanket, **do not** attempt to put it out. **GET OUT and call the fire brigade immediately**.
- **DO NOT** touch the fire blanket or anything underneath it until at least an hour has passed since the fire was extinguished.

Fire Blankets can also be used when exiting a burning building, wrap it around yourself for added protection if there are flames between you and the exit.

SAFETY TIPS

Ensure that everyone knows where the fire blanket is stored and knows how to remove the blanket from its canister should you ever need it. It is also recommended that an identification sign is displayed alongside the blanket.

6.4 FIRE ALARM

A **fire alarm system** is a set of electric/electronic devices/equipment working together to detect and alert people through visual and audio appliances when smoke/fire is present. These alarms may be activated from smoke detectors, heat detectors, water flow sensors, which are automatic or from a manual fire alarm pull station.

6.4.1 The parts of fire alarm system

- *Fire alarm control panel (FACP)* AKA fire alarm control unit (FACU); This component, the hub of the system, monitors inputs and system integrity, controls outputs and relays information.
- *Primary power supply*:Commonly the non-switched 120 or 240 Volt Alternating Current source supplied from a commercial power utility. In non-residential applications, a branch circuit is dedicated to the fire alarm system and its constituents. "Dedicated branch circuits" should not be confused with "Individual branch circuits" which supply energy to a single appliance.
- *Secondary (backup) power supplies*: This component, commonly consisting of sealed lead-acid storage batteries or other emergency sources including generators, is used to supply energy in the event of a primary power failure.

- *Initiating devices*: This component acts as an input to the fire alarm control unit and are either manually or automatically actuated. Examples would be devices pull stations, heat detectors, or smoke detectors. Heat and smoke detectors have different categories of both kinds. Some categories are beam, photoelectrical, aspiration, and duct.
- *Notification appliances*: This component uses energy supplied from the fire alarm system or other stored energy source, to inform the proximate persons of the need to take action, usually to evacuate. This is done by means of a flashing light, strobe light, electromechanical horn, "beeper horn", chime, bell, speaker, or a combination of these devices. The System Sensor Spectralert Advance Horn makes a beeping sound and electromechanical sound together.
- *Building safety interfaces*: This interface allows the fire alarm system to control aspects of the built environment and to prepare the building for fire, and to control the spread of smoke fumes and fire by influencing air movement, lighting, process control, human transport and exit.

6.5 HOSE REELS

A **fire hose** is a high-pressure hose that carries water or other fire retardant (such as foam) to a fire to extinguish it. Outdoors, it attaches either to a fire engine or a fire hydrant. Indoors, it can permanently attach to a building's standpipe or plumbing system.

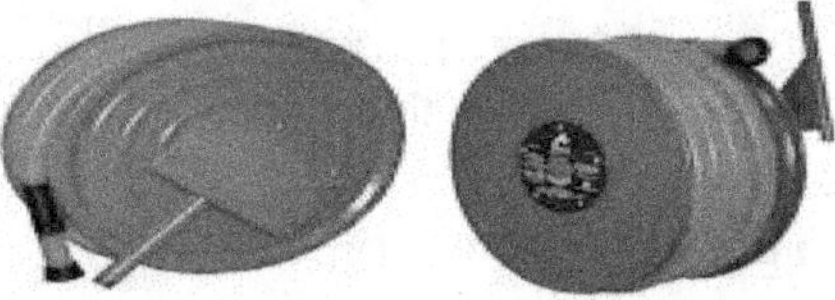

After use, a fire hose is usually hung to dry because standing water that remains in a hose for a long time can deteriorate the material and render it unreliable or unusable. Therefore, the typical fire station often has a high structure to accommodate the length of a hose for such preventative maintenance.

7.0 COMMON CAUSES OF FIRE

- Smoking and smoking materials
- Gas leakages
- Improper storage of flammables
- Heating appliances
- Open fires
- Unattended cooking
- Arson:- i. Gain
    - ii. Malice
    - iii. Revenge
    - iv. Pyromaniac
    - v. Juvenile vandals
- overheating of cooking gadgets
- overloading of electric gadgets

7.1 What to do in case of fire

- Raise an alarm by shouting fire, fire
- Stay out call the fire brigade.
- Fight fire at its initial stages, using the right fire extinguisher if safe to do so.
- Close doors and windows and do not lock.
- Evacuate the building in an orderly manner to avoid a stamped. Do not shout this may cause confusion to other people.
- Do not use lift or elevators
- Do not go back to collect your valuables.
- Do not go back to the building unless advised to do so by the fire brigade.
- Go to the fire assembly point for a roll call.

7.2 Basic rules for fighting fire

Fires can be very dangerous and you should always be certain that you will not endanger yourself or others when attempting to put out a fire.

For this reason, when a fire is discovered…

1. Assist any person in immediate danger to safety, if it can be accomplished without risk to yourself.
2. Call fire brigade or activate the building fire alarm. The fire alarm will notify the fire department and other building occupants and shut off the air handling system to prevent the spread of smoke.

If the fire is small (and Only after having done these 2 things), you may attempt to use an extinguisher to put it out.

However . . . .

. . . before deciding to fight the fire, keep these things in mind:

1. **Know what is burning.** If you don't know what's burning, you won't know what kind of extinguisher to use.
2. Even if you have an ABC fire extinguisher, there may be something in the fire that is going to explode or produce toxic fumes.
3. **Is the fire spreading** rapidly beyond the point where it started? The time to use an extinguisher is at the beginning stages of the fire.
4. If the fire is already spreading quickly, it is best to simply pull the fire alarm and evacuate the building.

Do <u>not</u> fight the fire if:

- ✓ **You don't have adequate or appropriate equipment.** If you don't have the correct type or large enough extinguisher, it is best not to try fighting the fire.
- ✓ **You might inhale toxic smoke.** When synthetic materials such as the nylon in carpeting or foam padding in a sofa burn, they can produce hydrogen cyanide, acrolein, and ammonia in addition to carbon monoxide. These gases can be fatal in very small amounts.
- ✓ **Your instincts tell you not to.** If you are uncomfortable with the situation for any reason, just let the fire department do their job.

The final rule is to always position yourself with an exit or means of escape at your back before you attempt to use an extinguisher to put out a fire.

In case the extinguisher malfunctions, or something unexpected happens, you need to be able to get out quickly. You don't want to become trapped.

7.3 The Emergency Procedure

If there is a fire in your building, please proceed to the nearest exit and leave in an orderly manner.

Remain outside until you are given the all clear by the fire or police department.

7.4 An Activity

During a fire evacuation operation using a helicopter the people below profiled, are trapped and you can only evacuate three people at a time. In order of priority select the three people you will evacuate:

John	–	A reverend father at the local church
Jezebel	–	A known prostitute in the same town.
Christine	–	Is pregnant with her first born
Millicent	–	A visiting granny to Christine
Timothy	–	Former Army officer
Daniel	–	Youth choir chairman at a local church

8.0 THE FAMOUS FIREMAN'S CARRY

In most scenarios in Kenyan fire emergency cases; there are no better tools and equipments in moving fire emergency casualties to safe zones. This is one of the oldest and most often used techniques to get an injured or unconscious person away from danger. The technique allows a person to carry another person on the shoulders without assistance. While the firefighters may seem superhuman, especially for untrained people, firefighters often employ this technique to maximize their strength and allow to do more in an emergency.

8.1 The steps to doing a fireman's carry

1. **Make sure that there is no possibility of spinal injury before moving the victim.** If a traumatic accident has taken place and you think the victim has injured his spine, then do not move him unless it's absolutely necessary to evade an urgent danger, such as a flood.
2. **Roll the victim onto his stomach if he's on his back.** If the victim is on his back, then you should roll him over on his stomach so he will be easier to lift.

To do this, just place one arm on the victim's shoulder and one arm on the same side of his body and push or pull him on to his stomach.

3. **Hook your elbows under his armpits.** To do this, kneel by the victim's head and hook your elbows under his shoulders, therefore sticking your arms under the person's back and armpits. Your head should be facing the victim's feet and you should have your feet planted on the ground so you can stand easily.

4. **Raise the victim to his feet.** Lift him slowly, using your legs to support the person's weight. Avoid using the strength of your back to lift the person, or you may injure yourself. Raise him until his feet are just a foot or so away from being straightened into standing position and are still dragging on the ground a bit.

5. **Place your right leg between the victim's legs.** This will help you get a firmer grip on the victim. Just move your weight to your right or dominant leg and stick it between the victim's legs for support. If your dominant leg is your left leg, then use your left leg instead and follow the opposite of all of the positioning in the instructions.

6. **Grab the victim's right hand with your left.** You should begin to do this *as* you place your right leg between the victim's legs. If your dominant leg is your right leg, then you should grab the victim's right hand with your left hand; if not, do the opposite. After you do that, you should drape the hand over your shoulder so you have more leverage, with your head planted under the victim's armpit and side.

7. **Squat down.** Keep your back as straight as possible when you do this. Place the victim's body over above your shoulders, so that his torso is relatively perpendicular to the ground. Try to distribute his weight as evenly as you can over your shoulders so that he doesn't tilt to one side.

8. **Wrap your right arm around the back of the victim's right knee.** To do this, put your right arm between the victim's legs to reach behind his right knee. This will help you get a firmer grasp on the victim. Your left hand should still be holding on to the victim's right hand. Gripping the victim with both hands on his knee and arm will help you lift him.

9. **Rise up and lift the victim's right thigh over your right shoulder.** Keep your back straight. The left leg and arm of the person should now be hanging behind and the body should be supported by your shoulders. Hold onto the victim's right arm and leg with your right and left hands, respectively, as you stand up. Alternately, you can use your right arm to wrap around the victim's thighs *and* grab his right hand.

10. **Move the victim.** Now that you have the victim draped safely over your back, you should look forward and move cautiously, using your free arm for balance. To do this, you'll need to adjust your weight. Gently adjust the weight to distribute evenly among both shoulders; this will enable you to carry the person for longer distances, possibly 50 feet (15 m) or more. Try to keep the victim's torso level to prevent further injury.

8.2 Applications

This method is also used by first responders who need to move someone from a dangerous situation such as lifeguards and police officers. The fireman's carry method has also been applied by the soldiers to move the wounded to safer ground, whether a fellow soldier or civilian. This technique has also been used in combat sports too; judo practitioners and professional wrestlers have both used a version of the fireman's carry to lift an opponent, especially one bigger and stronger than they are. With this technique, anyone can almost turn into a superhero.

8.3 Advantages

Carrying someone in this manner has several advantages over other methods of moving another person. The subject's torso is fairly level, which helps prevent further injuries. When the subject's weight is evenly distributed over both shoulders, it is easier to carry them for a longer distance - 50 feet or more.

The fireman's carry is preferred over a single-shoulder carry if someone is seriously hurt or if the person must be carried for a considerable amount of time. A person being carried over one shoulder would experience more jarring as his or her body is dangling more freely over the carrier's shoulder. Also, blood would be unevenly distributed if someone was dangling upside-down over the carrier's shoulder for an extended period of time. This could also be a very uncomfortable position for the carried person if he or she is still conscious.

8.4 Disadvantages of this technique

In firefighting, smoke and heat are greater higher up, and may be fatal to the person being carried. The person carried is largely outside the rescuer's field of vision, and almost all vital areas are out of the rescuer's view. Thus, dangerous changes in their condition can be missed, and an inexperienced rescuer can inadvertently create or further compound injuries via collision with obstacles. Furthermore, the rescuer's obstructed peripheral vision puts both persons at risk if the incident that caused the injury is still ongoing (fire, combat, public disturbances, etc.).

The fireman's carry, utilizing back and shoulder strength, is engineered as an emergency measure to optimize power, endurance, and mobility. As such, it may be applicable where there is ongoing hazard, the carried person is larger than the rescuer, the rescuer is otherwise unable to move the victim at all, or it is imperative to cross significant distances, quickly. It is by no means appropriate when a stretcher is available and a viable alternative, or when the rescuer has the size and strength to easily carry the subject in a gentler, more compassionate and considerate hold.

The fireman's carry presents severe hazards if the person being carried has or may have a spinal injury, and should be avoided except in immediate emergency.

9.0 THE COLD FIRE EXTINGUISHER TECHNOLOGY

The Kenyan fire industry is slowly transforming itself to embrace the latest technology in fire suppression systems. The latest entry in the market is the Cold Fire Extinguishing agents. This suppressing agent is completely environmental friendly. This means that the agent is green, non-toxic, non-corrosive and biodegradable. The product is a combination of plant extracts and water and is environmentally friendly; UL listed Wetting Agent for Class A and Class B fires, also works on Class D (metal) fires.

9.1 How does it work?

In order to under how Cold Fire extinguishers work, one must be able to understand the components of fire triangle. In order for a fire to be created, three components are necessary, fuel, oxygen, and heat. These three components form what is called a "Fire Triangle". Most agents extinguish fires by breaking down one leg of the fire triangle to stop the flame propagation. Cold Fire Extinguishers works to break down and remove 2 components from the fire triangle, heat and fuel. ColdFire is considered to have 6 times the penetrating capability of water. This characteristic, coupled with its extraordinary capability to absorb heat, allows the extinguisher to penetrate a fire faster, absorb the heat, and bring the fuel source generating the fire under its flashpoint more quickly. Cold Fire Extinguishers also works to simultaneously encapsulate the fuel source of the fire. It also works to encapsulate the fuels vapors and begins to break down the molecular structure of the hydrocarbon fuel source extinguishing the fire and preventing re-ignition.

9.2 Its Advantages

Cold Fire Suppression Systems offers many advantages over conventional fire suppressing systems:

- Flexible, narrow tubing enables it to be inserted into small narrow spaces
- No electricity required; it will work even in electrical failure
- Virtually no installation limitations
- Simple design reduces maintenance
- Always activates at hottest point of the fire
- Suppresses fire in seconds, minimizing damage
- Quick and simple installation
- The extinguishing agent minimizes damage

- Cost-effective and practical compared to other extinguishing systems
- Operational from 120 °F to -65 °F depending on Cold Fire Extinguisher fill
- Unaffected by moisture intrusion

10. INSURANCE AGAINST FIRE

Insurance against fire usually referred to as fire and related perils is slowly gaining preference in the Kenya industries with companies taking more keen interest in the cover. But what does it entail to have a fire cover against your premise?

Currently fire insurance accounts for a fairly high proportion of total non- life insurance premium income in Kenya. Many insurers treat fire as the main insurance business. Other classes of insurance are considered as "accommodation "business. The basic fire policy is called the standard fire policy because it covers same perils that is, fire, lightning, and limited explosion.

- **Fire:** Fire is the actual ignition of something that should not be on fire, the cause being accidental or fortuitous. There are exclusions under this peril however.
- **Lightning:** Any loss covered by lightning is covered under fire policy.
- **Explosion**: Explosion cover is limited to explosion of boilers or gases used for domestic purposes, the use, however, will determine if the boiler or gas is domestic. In this regard a boiler located in the factory but used to boil water for making tea or washing hands is regarded as domestic.

10.1 Special perils under fire policy
The standard fire policy may be extended to cover other perils which are classified and described here below.
Social perils
These are perils with human source and they include strikes, riots, malicious damage and civil commotion.
Chemical perils
Chemical perils include explosions and spontaneous fermentation or heating. The latter peril should be under written with care because:
- The property to be insured is usually prone to self jesting;
- if property self-ignites it is very difficult to extinguish the fire
- salvage prospects are low
- very careful control of storage is essential; and
- insurers will need to incur costs of survey before accepting the risk

Natural Perils Natural perils include:
- storm, that is atmospheric disturbances of unusual nature

- flood, that is, escape of water from the normal confines of any natural or artificial water works;
- earth quake;
- subterranean or underground fire or fire of volcanic nature; and
- subsidence, ground heave or land slip. Subsidence is uneven settlement of made up ground e.g. movement of foundations. Ground heave occur when ground that previously had low moisture is suddenly able to accept more moisture. A land slip is a min miniature land slide. It is a rapid movement down ward under the influence of gravity of a mass of rock or earth on a slope.
-

10.2 Miscellaneous perils

These are perils that cannot be classified under any of the above categories and are mainly escape of water, damage caused by any aerial device or articles dropped thereof and impact damage, especially to buildings caused by vehicles.

Long – term agreements under fire policies

This is where the insurer gives a premium discount in consideration of the insured offering to renew the contact for a given term, for example three or five years. The insured is under obligation to renew. Failure to do so will require that the insured pays back the enjoyed discount however, if the insurer changes the terms and conditions of the contract, the insured is not bound to renew.

Business Interruption Insurance

The policy is offered to protect future earnings of an enterprise after damage from an insured peril such as fire, including special perils. The fire and related perils policy (material damage) covers buildings and contents or the capital items of a business. The material damage policy does not cover loss of profits occasioned by fire or any other peril insured. This is only covered under the business interruption policy. The perils covered under the business interruption policy are the same as those covered under the material damage policy.

The most common business interruption policies are those that cover losses from
- Fire and special perils
- Computer damage and breakdown
- Engineering machinery breakdown

In a paraphrase, the purpose of business interruption insurance is to cover:
- Net profit which would otherwise have been earned;

- reimburse those standing charges or fixed expenses reduction in turn over or sales;
- Meet such additional costs as are insured to enable the business to recover more quickly to reduce the loss, for example, lease of alternative premises.

Its for this reason that companies should ensure that their workplace is insured against fire and eventuality.

<u>**THE FIREMAN'S PRAYER**</u>
When duty call's me, oh Lord,
Wherever Flames may rage,
Give me the strength to save some life
Whatever Be its age.

Help me embrace a little child
Before it is too late
Or save an older person from
The horror of that fate

Enable me to be alert,
and oh Lord, guide my every move,
for life is so precious,
please don't let us loose.

I want to fill my calling and
To give the best in me
To guard my every neighbor
And protect their property

And if according to thy will,
That I must give my life,
Then with thy protecting hand my Lord,
I pray thee, protect my children and my wife.

Amen

CBHW071241140726
47996CB00007B/2706

www.ingramcontent.com/pod-product-compliance
Lightning Source LLC
Chambersburg PA